Love Me
Till I Die

Daniel Schramm, D. Min.

TEACH Services, Inc.
P U B L I S H I N G
www.TEACHServices.com ● (800) 367-1844

Copyright © 2014 Daniel Schramm
Copyright © 2014 TEACH Services, Inc.
ISBN-13: 978-1-4796-0348-0 (Paperback)
ISBN-13: 978-1-4796-0349-7 (ePub)
ISBN-13: 978-1-4796-0350-3 (Mobi)

Published by

TEACH Services, Inc.
P U B L I S H I N G
www.TEACHServices.com • (800) 367-1844

Introduction

Time is fast fleeting for all of us, but if you are dying, time is of more value and each moment is precious since you don't know how much longer you have with those you love. However, sometimes it is difficult to express your desires or feelings during this time of uncertainty. This booklet is written to help facilitate a conversation with those you love or those who are caring for you at the end of your life.

If you are caring for a loved one who is dying, despite your feelings of overwhelming stress and sadness, there are many things you can do. This booklet offers helpful tips and ideas of what you can do to help your loved one be comfortable and peacefully say goodbye.

In my diverse international experience of twenty-five years serving as a pastor, chaplain, and professor, I have been with numerous dying individuals and have observed that these amazing people and their loved ones are often caught by surprise. And the ones who don't have any regrets are those who maximize every moment to give and receive love. I want this booklet to teach people how to maximize love for those who are dying and minimize the regrets for those who are left behind.

Love Me Till I Die

Listen to My Feelings and Wishes About Dying

My life is almost over. I feel stunned. People who get into a fatal accident, drop dead of a heart attack, or die in their sleep are here one minute and gone the next. They don't experience the fear, sadness, and pain that I am enduring. I know I am dying. I have time to think about my human journey coming to an end. I have time to contemplate my life and what I am leaving behind.

Death used to seem like a distant event that happened to someone else. However, death is staring me in the face, and I am afraid. However, I know I am not the only one who is scared. I know it is hard for you to see me decline. I realize that you are worried about me. I also realize that as you watch me decline in health, you are thinking about your own demise. This is only natural, but it leaves both of us emotionally raw.

Even though I may wear a brave face or say that everything is fine, I need you to walk beside me as I near the end. Dying makes me long to be loved and listened to more than ever before. My final wish is to love you without reserve and feel your love in return until I take my last breath. It may seem selfish to ask you to love me so much, especially if we have had our differences, yet love will strengthen the bond between us and heal any wounds that may be festering.

Please listen to me; in return, I will listen to you. There is wisdom in this quote by Ralph Nichols: "The most basic of all human needs is the need to understand and be understood. The best way to understand people is to listen to them."[1] Please listen to me, especially now that I am dying. Listen to me reminisce about my childhood or my favorite hobby or a cherished family memory. Listen to me talk about my feelings, my fears, and my reaction to the news. Continue to listen to me as I share with you my desires and my struggles as I live out my final days. In exchange, let me extend to you the gift of listening.

Understand That I Feel Stressed

It is an emotional rollercoaster to know that you are dying and wonder when it will happen. You know it is coming, but no one can tell you exactly how much longer you have on this earth. At varying times and degrees, my emotions range from that of anger, sadness, joy, disappointment, gratitude, confusion, and acceptance. These feelings are compounded by my physical pain and decreased energy. I do not intend to take out my frustrations on you, but please understand that the stress I am under causes me to snap at times. I love you dearly and do not want to say or do anything to hurt you, but dying is stressful, and sometimes I speak without thinking.

---

1   Ralph Nichols, professor emeritus of rhetoric, University of Minnesota, made this statement in a paper titled "The Struggle to be Human," which was presented at an academic convention in Atlanta, Georgia, on February 17, 1980.

Don't Hide From Me

I am not blind to the fact that this is also an emotional rollercoaster for you and that you, too, are dealing with your own stress in relation to my health. I'm sure you feel overwhelmed at times and do not know what to do or how to relate. When we don't know what to do, it is natural to remove ourselves from the situation. However, please deny your natural inclination to distance yourself from me. Please do not hide, regardless of our past or your fear. If you live nearby, please come see me. If you live far away, please call me. Rather than hiding, please come even closer.

When we talk, whether in person or via the phone, share your feelings with me, laugh with me, cry with me, and listen to me express my feelings. I would even welcome you sharing your sadness with me—there is no need to act strong. Avoid acting happy if you are depressed or angry. Not only can you hide from me physically by not visiting or calling, you can hide from me by masking your emotions. Please don't do this. Don't worry about doing or saying the wrong things, simply love me. As George Sand said, "There is only one happiness in life, to love and be loved."[2] Don't hide from this chance to draw nearer to me. You can start by simply telling me you love me—love will help soothe the stress.

Notice What Makes Me Feel Loved

Although our time together may be short, take whatever time we have left together to learn more about me. Ask me what communicates love to me. Ask others who know me well to share insights as to what they have done over

---

2   "George Sand," Wikipedia, http://1ref.us/8 (accessed May 20, 2014).

the years to show me love. If you have the time, take it one step further and read about the five love languages that speak to different people. Learn about what makes me feel loved[3], and then shower me with those things.

Accept Outside Help

To better understand the emotions I will experience as I prepare to die, I encourage you to seek professional guidance from a counselor, mentor, pastor, social worker, medical professional, or hospice nurse. Most specifically, hospice nurses specialize in caring for people who are dying. I have heard that these nurses are dedicated to supporting families and making the dying person comfortable. Hospice's services are covered by insurance or Medicaid/Medicare, so please do not hesitate to enlist their assistance. Professional input could alleviate some of your stress, which in the end will result in better care for me.

Accept Me and My Medical Condition

I need you to accept the fact that I am dying. I need you to accept my terminal medical condition and my healthcare decisions. I no longer want heroic interventions. I have fought heroically to live, but now I ask you to join me in accepting that this is my time to die. However, this acceptance does not mean that I want to stop living while I am still alive. While coming to terms with my death, until that day comes, let's keep on living. Time is a precious gift, and I want to make the most of what time is left. We can't change the inevitable, but once we accept that, we can enjoy the time that we do have together.

---

3   Gary Chapman, *The Five Love Languages* (Chicago, IL: Northfield Publishing, 2007)

Help Me Live in the Now . . .

Help me focus on today. "But few of us live in the present. Having a life-threatening illness takes away our future and glorifies our past. It gives us the opportunity to live in the present..."[4] My terminal condition is a reminder that this day is sacred and may be the last one we share together. Each day is a gift, and we must live it to the fullest, cherishing the moments that we do have.

I understand that it is uncomfortable to discuss death, yet this is my reality, and sometimes I need to talk about it. Please do not leave me to face my mortality alone. I feel lonely when you are in denial. Be emotionally aware that, while I am striving to live each day to the fullest, I am still dying, and I can't completely ignore or bury that fact.

As I endeavor to live in the here and now, there are some practical things you can do to increase my quality of life. I hope that doing some of these things will also help you to get rid of your feelings of helplessness. You do not need to follow all of these suggestions, yet some of them will help us enhance our remaining time together.

... Beautify My Living Space

Please make my living space as neat, clean, and beautiful as possible. Kindly get rid of clutter so I can enjoy the simplicity of my favorite things. Place a cozy chair in my bedroom or in the living room where I can relax during the day. Arrange the furniture to face a window so that I can drink in the beauty of the outdoors. If there are no flowers or birds outside for my window, please hang a bird feeder or a potted plant near my window. I want to enjoy pretty things both inside and outside my room.

---

4   Barbara Karnes, A *Time to Live: Living With a Life-Threatening Illness* (Vancouver, WA: Barbara Karnes Books, 1996), p. 2.

Please display a few of my favorite photos and personal items in my room. Candles or room fresheners add a special touch as long as the fragrance is not overwhelming. Fresh flowers also brighten any room. I would much prefer receiving flowers while I am alive and can enjoy them versus you saving them for the funeral. Beautify my living space regardless if I am at home or in a hospital, nursing home, personal care home, or another facility.

... *Share Music With Me*

I want music to grace my environment. Music can bring peace to a soul, transporting the listener to another time and place in one's life. I long to dwell on the good memories of my past, and music can help facilitate that. Furthermore, music offers comfort and peace. When selecting music, consider the time of day, my mood, and my needs. I may want something lively to wake me up in the morning or something soothing to help me sleep. Some days I will want to listen to what I played when I was younger. At other times, I will prefer spiritual or classical music. If you don't remember what I like, please ask me what music I want to listen to. Beyond listening to music by myself, I would love to listen with you and share some of my favorite songs with you.

In addition to listening to music, please ask me what music I want at my memorial service. Ask me what my favorite hymn is or if I have any other sacred songs that I love to listen to.

... *Treat Me Like I Can Still Hear You*

Despite what you may think, I not only hear music, but I also hear you. I understand that sometimes it looks like I am sleeping or half out of it because of the medication I am on, but hearing is usually the last sense to remain before someone passes away. Thus, refrain from dehumanizing me by speaking to others as if I am already gone. Also, please do not speak poorly of me or complain about me while I am in the room, because I hear everything you say, and your words can hurt me deeply. You may think that whispering is better, but it is worse. I wonder if you are pitying me or hiding things from me. I wonder if you are secretly discussing my condition or are finding fault with me and how I am dealing with dying. So please treat me like I can still hear, even if you think I am asleep.

... Talk With Me

Talk openly with me. I want to reminisce about our life experiences together. If I can no longer speak because I am tired or in pain, please share stories with me. It may seem strange to have a one-sided conversation, but your voice will take my mind off of my pain or fear. Tell me about your favorite memories of us. Tell me what you will always remember about me. Tell me what you appreciate about me. Tell me what you love about me; in fact, use the word "love" liberally. I will not tire of hearing you say, "I love you." And you will not regret speaking those three powerful words. Express love to me every way you can, whether it is through kind deeds, gifts, physical touch, time, or encouraging words, including love notes, cards, or poems.

"Love me till I die.
Love me without asking why.
Love me for no reason.

Love me every season.
Love me for my uniqueness.
Love me hard, love me endless.
Love me for my cute charm.
Love me, hold my arm,
Never let go, just love me.
Oh, love me!"[5]

... Pray With Me

As I prepare to say goodbye to this earthly life, my mind may be unsettled as I contemplate my eternal destiny. Please be open to my spiritual needs and be willing to pray with me if I so desire. If I express an interest in talking with a spiritual leader, please help arrange for such a meeting. This is my last opportunity to make things right in my life. Please don't take this lightly. Please help me to process my feelings so that I am at peace with myself, others, and God when I die.

In addition to praying with me, please pray for me. Pray that I may experience peace and a calm assurance of God's presence as I near the end. Be aware that I may shed tears of appreciation as you pray, but don't let this stop you from praying for me, especially each time you leave.

If you do not feel comfortable praying, you could read prayers such as:

"God, grant me the serenity to accept the things I cannot change, the courage to

---

5   Gabor Timis, Canmore, Canada, original poem written on September 12, 2012.

change the things I can and the wisdom to know the difference ..."[6]

"Lord, make me an instrument of your peace. Where there is hatred, let me sow love; where there is injury, pardon; ... where there is despair, hope; where there is darkness, light; and where there is sadness, joy ..."[7]

... Please Touch Me

More than words, I need your touch. Just as studies have shown that babies can actually die from lack of touch,[8] I can too at this time of my life. As I decline, words will become less important and touch more prominent. Please be gentle as I may be in pain, but touch me on the shoulder as you sit near my bedside. Hold my hand as we walk, talk, or pray together. Caress my hair as you care for my appearance. Touch eases my pain, loneliness, and anxiety. Medical care can be impersonal. I need your touch to help me feel like I am cherished and loved.

---

6   Reinhold Niebuhr first spoke this prayer in a sermon in 1943. It was then written in a booklet for Army chaplains in 1944. Today, this prayer has been widely adopted by Alcoholics Anonymous and other twelve-step programs.

7   Although this quote is commonly attributed to St. Francis of Assisi, who lived in the thirteenth century, scholars debate the validity of his authorship.

8   Dr. Ben Benjamin is one of many physicians who have documented in scientific research that babies waste away and die when deprived of human touch. In an article published in *Health Touch News* on August 31, 2013, Dr. Benjamin states that in one study a hundred years ago 99 percent of babies died in orphanages when deprived of human touch.

Hugs are a magical form of touch that will comfort both of us. "Almost instinctively in a time of crisis, we hug one another. Why? "Physical touch is a powerful communicator of love."[9] Even if I have not been into hugs, I may be now. I would welcome a hug when you come to see me, in the middle of a story, when I cry, or when I simply ask you for one.

... Be Authentic With Me

I want to finish life being real. Help me to open up and become vulnerable. We may need to have some overdue conversations about difficult topics, but I do not want to die with regrets, and I do not want you to live the rest of your life wishing you could have talked to me about something that was bothering you. Dying has increased my desire for forgiveness, reconciliation, and peace. So, let's talk seriously, and if needed, apologize to one another. Authenticity brings closeness, and I long for closeness without walls or barriers.

... Help Me Let Go of Guilt

If we have apologized for past disagreements, let's simply let them go. Time is too short to stay angry with one another, be hurt, or pull away. However, while I want you to be real with me, I do not need you to pile on the guilt over my mistakes and shortcomings. I am already feeling guilty and beating myself up over my past failures. I do not need you to harp on me about my character flaws. Instead, I need you to help me let go of the past by telling me it is OK to leave the guilt behind.

---

9   Gary Chapman, *The Five Love Languages* (Chicago, IL: Northfield Publishing, 2007), p. 64.

Consider the following poem written to eulogize a beloved husband who was similar to all of us—flawed, yet precious. "When I come to the end of my journey and I travel my last weary mile ... remember only the smile. Forget unkind words I have spoken; remember some good I have done ... and remember I have had loads of fun."[10] As we say goodbye, let's minimize guilt and maximize love.

(If abuse is involved, serious steps may need to be taken to address the emotions of all affected parties. It is best to seek the assistance of a professional in dealing with this type of closure.)

... Have Fun With Me

Laughter is like medicine to me. When I am laughing and having fun, my stress level plummets. I'd love to hear your favorite jokes or stories again. Tell me something amusing, or read me a funny story. I desire to feel pleasure and enjoyment during this difficult time. Maybe we can watch a funny movie together, even if we can only watch parts of the movie at a time. You also know what games I like to play. But please don't go easy on me; I want to win fair and square. Regardless of what entertainment we enjoy together, remember that I want to laugh and have a good time, just like you.

... Surprise Me

Dying can be very boring, especially when dealing with a terminal illness that stretches on and on. Surprise me by breaking up the monotony of my days. I'd love to hear from a former neighbor, teacher, or coworker. It would be a

---

10 This is an excerpt from a poem written by Lyman Hancock, an elderly Iowa farmer's wife, as a eulogy for her husband of almost sixty years.

joy to read the comics from the newspaper or look through old photos, souvenirs, or other belongings. Surprise me with special food or activities on special occasions such as birthdays, anniversaries, and holidays. Be creative and minimize boredom. Realize that while I may not be able to venture out to enjoy these simple pleasures, I would love for you to bring them to me.

... Respect My Privacy

I need rest, down time, and privacy. I may not tell you this, so study my body language to determine when I need space. I recognize that this is draining on you too. Please live your life and guard your health and your career. Feel free to take trips and get away. Other people can care for me; it is not necessary for you to be with me all the time. The key is that when you are with me, you are really with me. It also helps me to know when you will visit and when you will be away.

The more introverted I am, the more privacy I need. Allow me to talk alone with others who visit. I want to say goodbye individually to all of my loved ones. I need a balance of your company and privacy during this time.

Guard every aspect of my privacy, including my final requests and desires for my funeral. I want to relax, knowing you will follow my instructions regarding my medical care, funeral service, possessions, and private information. Thank you for respecting my dying wishes.

... Accept My Blessing Upon Your Life

I am very sorry if you have not previously felt my full support. I wish I could change the past. I wish I would have loved you more. However, my focus is now on you and your future. I want you to experience success, love, and happiness. Before dying, I may wish to place my hands upon you and bless you. Please carry my blessing into your future, despite what may have happened between us in the past.

If you are my spouse, you have my blessing to re-marry. Remember what we shared, but know that I want you to experience physical touch and every form of love that I can no longer give. If you are my child, know that you have my enthusiastic support to follow your dreams.

I want you to feel my love for you so that when I am gone, you will remember how much you meant to me and how much I valued our time together.

As we part, may you experience this old Irish blessing: "May the road rise up to meet you. May the wind be always at your back. May the sun shine warm upon your face. May the rains fall soft upon your fields, and until we meet again, may God hold you in the palm of His hand."[11]

Thank You for Loving Me

I am deeply grateful that you have chosen to love me until the end. Thank you for implementing some of the things I have suggested. Once I am gone, please do not beat yourself up or question your care for me. The care you have given me has made me feel loved and has helped me to peacefully say goodbye. May you live the rest of your life loving those around you and being loved in return.

---

11   Some attribute this traditional Irish blessing to St. Patrick, a fifth century church bishop from Ireland; however, others believe its origin is unknown.

We invite you to view the complete
selection of titles we publish at:

www.TEACHServices.com

Scan with your mobile
device to go directly
to our website.

Please write or e-mail us your praises, reactions, or
thoughts about this or any other book we publish at:

TEACH Services, Inc.
P U B L I S H I N G
www.TEACHServices.com ● (800) 367-1844

P.O. Box 954
Ringgold, GA 30736

info@TEACHServices.com

TEACH Services, Inc., titles may be purchased in bulk for
educational, business, fund-raising, or sales promotional use.
For information, please e-mail:

BulkSales@TEACHServices.com

Finally, if you are interested in seeing
your own book in print, please contact us at

publishing@TEACHServices.com

We would be happy to review your manuscript for free.

CPSIA information can be obtained at www.ICGtesting.com
Printed in the USA
LVOW12s2007230714

395369LV00021B/225/P